Science Builders

ELECTRICAL ENGINEERING

LEARN IT, TRY IT!

by Ed Sobey

CAPSTONE PRESS
a capstone imprint

Dabble Lab Books are published by Capstone Press,
1710 Roe Crest Drive, North Mankato, Minnesota 56003
www.mycapstone.com

Library of Congress Cataloging-in-Publication Data
Library of Congress Cataloging-in-Publication data is available on the Library of Congress website.
ISBN 978-1-5157-6426-7 (library binding)
ISBN 978-1-5157-6431-1 (paperback)
ISBN 978-1-5157-6438-0 (eBook PDF)

Editorial Credits
Mandy Robbins, editor; Steve Mead, designer; Kelli Lageson, media researcher; Laura Manthe, production specialist

Photo Credits
Capstone Studio: Karon Dubke, cover (bottom right), back cover, 9 (top and bottom), 10 (top and bottom), 11, 12, 16, 17
(top and bottom), 22, 23, 25 (back), 26, 27 (left, top right, bottom right), 32 (all), 33 (top and bottom), 34 (all), 36, 37 (top,
middle, bottom), 38 (top and bottom), 42 (top and bottom), 43 (top and bottom); Shutterstock: Africa Studio, 20, Aleksandr
Pobedimskiy, 15 (top), AlexRoz, 5, Alina Cardiae Photography, cover (top right), azure1, 25 (top left), Cesarz, 25 (bottom
left), cigdem, 6, CrackerClips Stock Media, 40, Everett Historical, 7 (left), Fouad A. Saad, 15 (bottom), Fresnel, 31, Garsya,
18, goir, 24, Jan Schneckenhaus, 19, Kim Reinick, 21, Perutskyi Petro, 25 (top right), Pixeljoy, 39, racorn, 4, Rawpixel.
com, 44, revers, 14, Ruud Morijn Photographer, 28, Scanrail1, cover (bottom left), Sergey Nivens, 7 (right), Svetlana
Serebryakova, 25 (bottom right), Tungphoto, 30, ULKASTUDIO, cover (top left)

Design elements: Shutterstock

Printed in the United States of America.
122017   010999R

TABLE OF CONTENTS

CHAPTER 1

WHAT DO ELECTRICAL ENGINEERS DO?

Look at all the machines in your house that use electricity. There are computers, televisions, and lights. They may be plugged into an electrical socket in the wall, or they may use batteries. Either way, electrical engineers helped to make each one. Electrical engineers design, build, and fix machines that use electricity.

How many electrical devices can you spot in this kitchen?

There are many different types of electrical engineering. Some engineers work on improving how electricity is made or delivered to your home. Others design electric motors or the electrical systems in computers. Some specialize in medical equipment. If designing or testing electrical devices sounds like fun, electrical engineering could be the field for you. But you don't have to wait to get started.

WHAT IS ELECTRICITY?

Electricity is the flow of **electrons** or electrical charge. Lightning is an example of a natural electric flow. Electrical charges move along materials called **conductors**. Many metals conduct electricity. Electrical engineers learn how to harness the power of electricity and make it do useful work.

Electrical cords contain metal wires that conduct electricity.

electron—a tiny particle in an atom that travels around the nucleus

conductor—a material that lets heat, electricity, or sound travel easily through it

BE SAFE AND HAVE FUN

Electrical engineering is fun and interesting, but electricity is a powerful force. Be sure to follow these safety rules when conducting experiments:

1

Ask an adult before you start doing experiments with electricity. With electricity comes the risk of electrical shocks and fire. Adult supervision is a must.

2

Only use batteries as your source of electricity. Never use electricity from an outlet. It is too strong and could severely hurt you or start a fire.

3

If you notice batteries or other parts getting hot, disconnect the batteries. Excessive heat suggests there is a "short circuit." This happens when one terminal of the battery is connected directly to the other terminal. In a short circuit, electricity speeds through the circuit. The batteries and wires get so hot that the batteries might be ruined.

EDISON

Thomas Edison was one of America's greatest inventors. He was kicked out of public school at the age of 11 for being hyperactive. Edison's mother was a schoolteacher, so she continued his education at home. There his curiosity pushed him to greatness. Edison performed many experiments with electricity. Much of today's technology can trace its roots back to Edison's inventions. These include improvements in electric light bulbs, batteries, and video cameras.

MAKE A CIRCUIT

The electrical circuit is the basis of electrical engineering. It is the path electricity moves along. Closing and opening a circuit turns electrical devices on and off. A closed circuit is on, and an open circuit is off.

Electronic stores and hobby stores carry all the supplies you need to create your own circuit. Battery holders that hold up to 4 AA batteries will make connecting batteries to circuits easier. LEDs are sold in small packs or bags. You will probably break some, so you'll need a whole pack. You will want a handful of clip leads. These are wires with clips at each end. Get the shortest length leads available.

If you can't take a trip to the hobby store, all of the items you need can be ordered online from science catalogs and electronic supply stores. Be sure to ask an adult for help.

MATERIALS

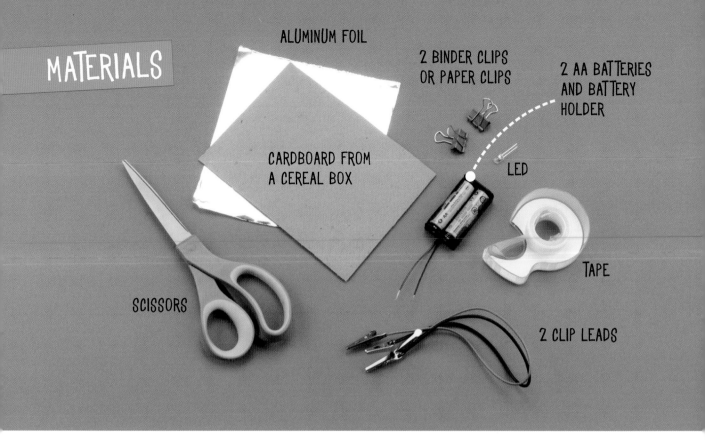

ALUMINUM FOIL

2 BINDER CLIPS
OR PAPER CLIPS

2 AA BATTERIES
AND BATTERY
HOLDER

CARDBOARD FROM
A CEREAL BOX

LED

TAPE

SCISSORS

2 CLIP LEADS

STEPS

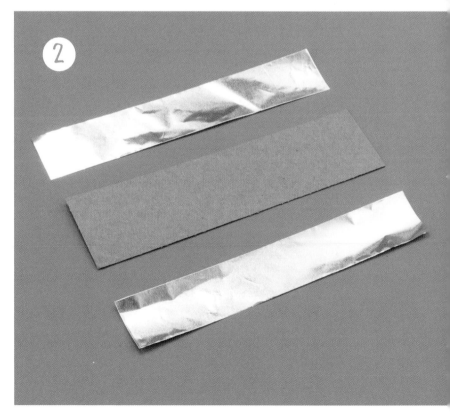

2

1. Cut a rectangle of cereal box cardboard 1.5 inches (4 centimeters) wide and 3 inches (8 cm) long.

2. Cut two strips of aluminum foil 3 inches (8 cm) long and 1 inch (2.5 cm) wide.

3 Wrap each strip around the long edge of the cardboard. Tape the
   strips in place if they won't stay in place. This simple circuit board will
   let you connect lights, motors, and batteries together.

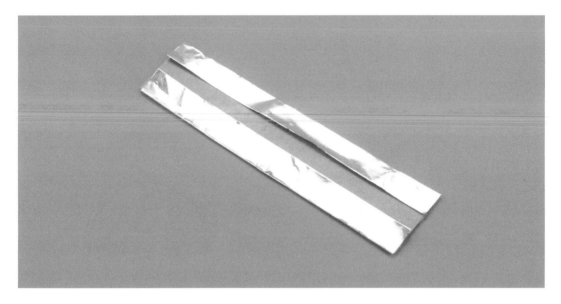

4 Connect an LED to the circuit board. Do this by gently bending the
   LED legs so each leg touches one of the two strips of aluminum foil.
   The two legs are not the same length.

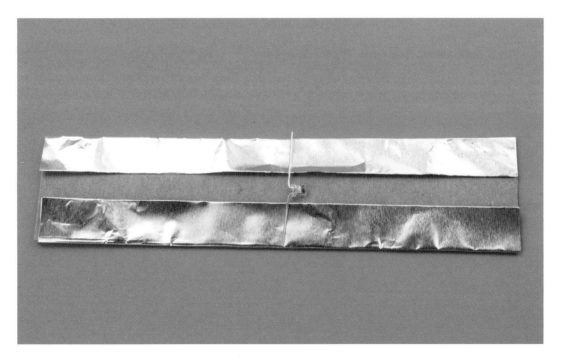

5. The longer leg connects to the positive terminal of the battery, so remember which leg is the longer one. Use binder clips to hold each leg onto the foil.

6. Mark the sides of the circuit board with a positive and negative symbol. Put the positive symbol on the side with the longer leg of the LED.

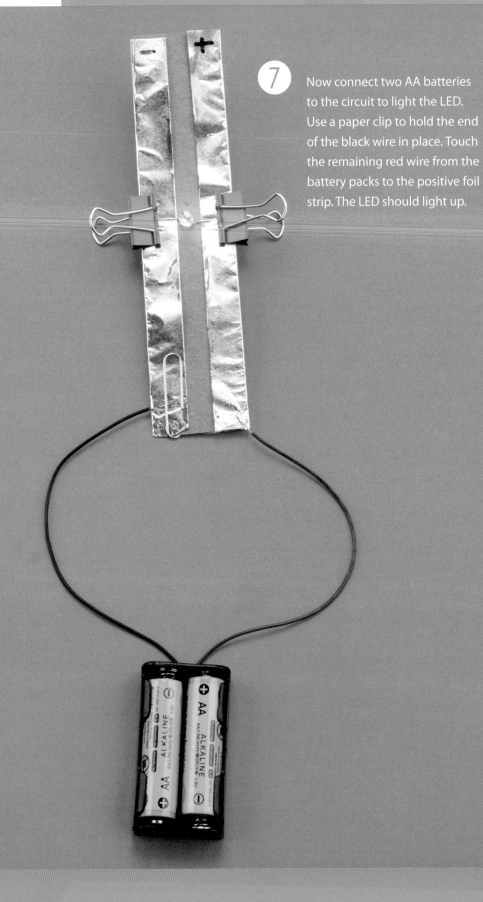

7 Now connect two AA batteries to the circuit to light the LED. Use a paper clip to hold the end of the black wire in place. Touch the remaining red wire from the battery packs to the positive foil strip. The LED should light up.

WHAT HAPPENED?

When you touched the red wire to the foil, electrons flowed from the two batteries through the circuit and the LED. The foil, wires, and LED legs are all metal conductors. If you touch the red wire to the cardboard the LED won't light. Cardboard is an **insulator**.

SERIES CIRCUITS

A series circuit has only one path for electrons to follow, either along the negative or positive charge. LED lights only work in a series circuit. That's why you had to connect the long leg of the LED to the positive battery connection. You can test this for yourself. Try switching the LED around so the long leg is connected to the negative battery terminal. Then connect the short side to the positive side. Does the LED light?

insulator—a substance that prevents or reduces the passage of electricity
volt—a unit for measuring the force of an electrical current or the stored power of a battery

CHAPTER 2

MAGNETISM

You probably know that magnets attract some metals. But did you know that magnets and electricity are connected? When electrons move, their electrical current makes a magnet. On the flip side, when a magnet moves it can create an electrical current. Electrical engineers use electrical and magnetic forces to make machines do work.

The magnets you are probably familiar with are permanent magnets. Perhaps you've played with them in science class or used them to stick your artwork to the refrigerator. These magnets are made of metal and don't need to be switched on or off. They are always magnetic.

In addition to permanent magnets, there are electromagnets. These are magnets you can turn on and off by powering them with electricity. One example of a simple electromagnet is called a **solenoid**. This type of electromagnet is made up of a metal rod wrapped in wire that conducts electricity. When the wire-wrapped rod is connected to an electrical source, it becomes an electromagnet. The more the wire covers the metal rod, the stronger the magnet will be.

FACT

Ancient people found "lodestones," which are naturally occurring magnets. They learned to use them for navigational compasses. Lodestones are made of the mineral magnetite. Scientists think lightning may have made them magnetic.

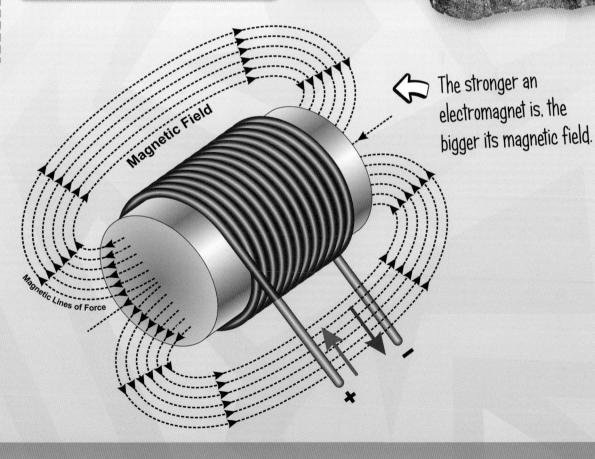

Magnetic Field

Magnetic Lines of Force

The stronger an electromagnet is, the bigger its magnetic field.

+

–

MAKE AN ELECTROMAGNET

Try making your own solenoid by wrapping a conducting wire around a metal nail. Each end of the nail will serve as the magnet's **poles**. As the electric current travels through a conducting wire, it creates a magnet. When you connect the electromagnet to the circuit board, the electrons start flowing. The magnet comes to life. When you disconnect the circuit, the magnet stops.

MATERIALS

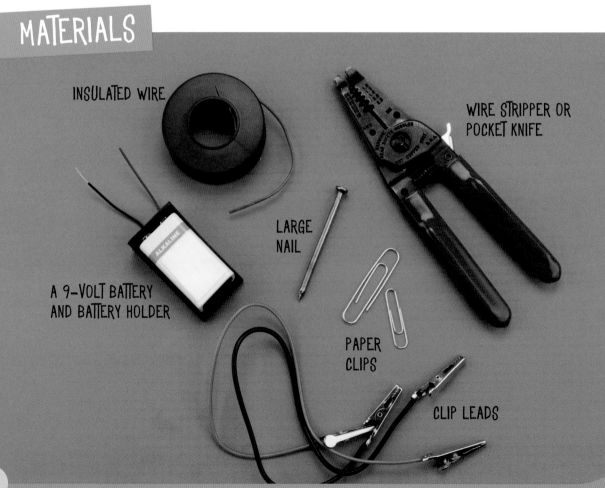

INSULATED WIRE

WIRE STRIPPER OR POCKET KNIFE

LARGE NAIL

A 9-VOLT BATTERY AND BATTERY HOLDER

PAPER CLIPS

CLIP LEADS

ALKALINE

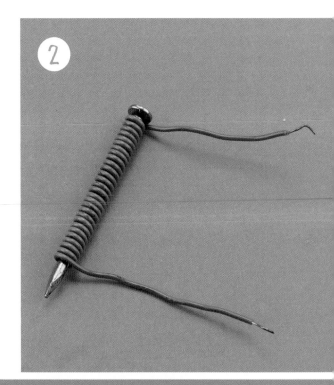

1 Cut 2 feet (0.6 meter) of wire. Ask an adult to remove 1 inch (2.5 cm) of insulation from each end of the wire. He or she can use a wire stripper or a pocket knife.

2 Wrap the wire tightly and neatly around the nail as many times as you can. You will need to connect the two uninsulated ends of the wire to a battery case, so make sure the ends don't get buried. The more you cover the nail with wire, the stronger your electromagnet will be.

3 Use clip leads to connect the two ends of the wire to the 9-volt battery. Hold the electromagnet above a pile of metal paper clips. Does it pick up the paper clips?

pole—one of the two ends of a magnet

SEEING MAGNETISM

Would you like to see your electromagnet's power? If you have a directional compass, you can see the power of your electromagnet's magnetic field. Compasses detect magnetic pulls. They typically point toward Earth's magnetic north pole. From there, people can figure out which direction east, west, and south are. But another magnetic force can interfere with that pull if it's placed near the compass. Put your compass near the electromagnet you've created. Connect the electromagnet to the battery and watch the needle of the compass. Hold the compass in different places around the electromagnet to watch the needle turn. This shows that the electricity flowing through the wire is creating a magnetic force.

HOW DOES AN ELECTRIC BUZZER WORK?

Electric buzzers have electromagnets inside. When you push the button, you close the circuit. This lets the electrons flow through the circuit. The current creates an electromagnet. It pulls the clapper to hit the bell inside the buzzer. As the clapper moves, it opens the circuit. That stops the current. With no more current flowing, the magnet weakens. A spring attached to the clapper pulls it back to its starting place. But if you keep your finger on the buzzer, the circuit will close again, pulling the clapper once again. The buzzer keeps ringing as long as you are pushing the button.

BUZZZZ!!!!

CHAPTER 3

HEAT AND MOTION

Electrical engineers have found all sorts of ways to harness the power of electricity. They use it to light things up and make sound. But that's not all! They also use it to make heat or cause motion.

Electric stove tops convert electricity to heat.

How does electricity create heat? As electricity moves through conductors, electrons bump into **atoms** in the conductors. Some of the energy created from the bumping is transformed into heat. The more a material **resists** the flow of electrons, the more energy is converted to heat. Take your toaster, for example. The curly metal wires in your toaster are called heating elements. They conduct electricity but have high resistance. The resistance is so high that as the electrical current flows through them, they get red hot. Their heat toasts your bread. Peek into the toaster the next time you're using it. You'll see electricity at work. Just be careful not to touch the inside or stick anything in there other than your toast.

Electrical engineers make and use electric motors to get different objects moving. Some cars use electric motors to drive the wheels. Electric pencil sharpeners have small electric motors. So do electric toothbrushes. If a machine moves and is powered by electricity, it has an electric motor.

atom—an element in its smallest form

resist—to oppose or slow the motion of an object

POWER AN ELECTRIC MOTOR

You can use the circuit board you made in the first project to power an electric toy motor. Small toy motors can be found at hobby or electronics stores.

MATERIALS

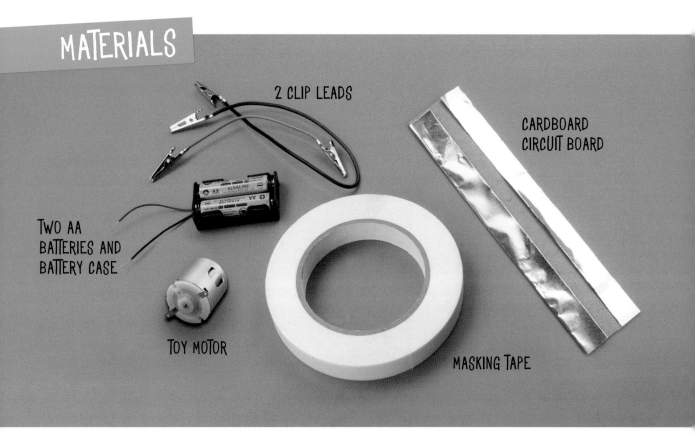

2 CLIP LEADS

CARDBOARD CIRCUIT BOARD

TWO AA BATTERIES AND BATTERY CASE

TOY MOTOR

MASKING TAPE

STEPS

1. Use the circuit board you made in Project 1. Remove the LED.

2 The toy motor should have two metal tabs called terminals. Use clip leads to connect them to the circuit board. Clip one lead to each side. Then connect the batteries to the circuit board as you did in the first project.

3 The metal post sticking up from the motor is its shaft. Is the motor shaft spinning? If you want to see it better, disconnect the batteries and put a small piece of masking tape on the shaft. Then reconnect the batteries.

4 What do you think will happen if you connect the battery wires to opposite sides of the circuit board? Will the motor still spin? Try it.

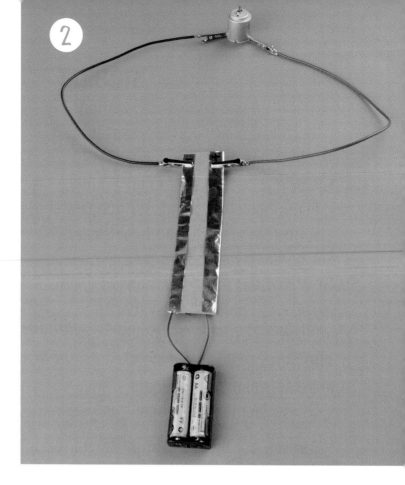

WHAT HAPPENED?

Why does the motor spin? If you've played with magnets you know that the positive pole of one magnet will attract the negative pole of another. That's what happens inside the motor. One set of magnets has permanent metal magnets. The other set has electromagnets. The magic of electric motors is that there is a switch inside that changes the electromagnet. If the electromagnet didn't change, the two magnets would hold each other in place. As it switches, the electromagnet is constantly pulled toward the permanent magnet and keeps the motor spinning.

When you switched the battery leads, the motor spun in the opposite direction. This happened because you changed the direction of the electric current.

CHAPTER 4

CONDUCTORS, INSULATORS, AND RESISTORS

Electrical engineers use parts called **resistors** when they need to reduce the current in a circuit. You can make your own resistor with a simple wooden pencil. The material inside a wooden pencil conducts electricity but has fairly high resistance. It is a mixture of graphite or carbon and other materials that help hold the graphite together.

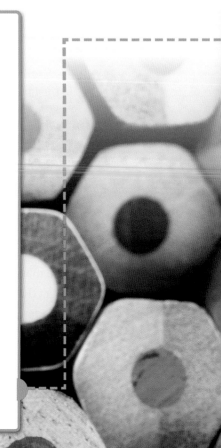

You can use the circuit board you built to test materials to see if they conduct electricity. From the first project, you know that aluminum foil conducts electricity. So do the metal wires inside the clip leads. But the rubber insulator on the outside of the clip leads does not. If you aren't sure if a material is a conductor, test it. Insert it into the circuit board. If your motor runs with a new material looped in, it's a conductor. If it doesn't, it is an insulator.

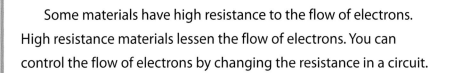

Some materials have high resistance to the flow of electrons. High resistance materials lessen the flow of electrons. You can control the flow of electrons by changing the resistance in a circuit.

resistor—a tool or device that slows down the flow of electrons in a circuit with a resistant material

MAKE A RESISTOR

Use the circuit board, batteries, clip leads, and electric motor from the previous project. Do you remember how fast the motor spun? Now watch how fast it spins when you add the pencil resistor into the circuit.

MATERIALS

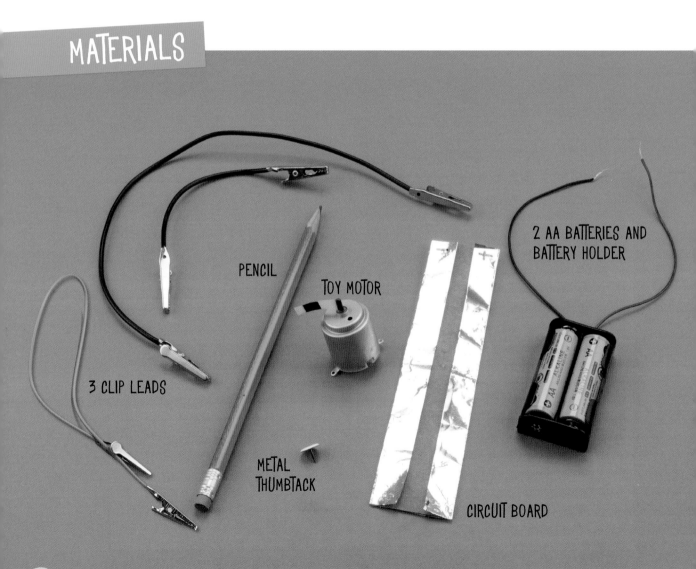

3 CLIP LEADS

PENCIL

TOY MOTOR

METAL THUMBTACK

CIRCUIT BOARD

2 AA BATTERIES AND BATTERY HOLDER

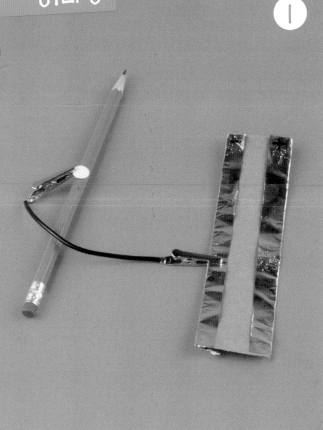

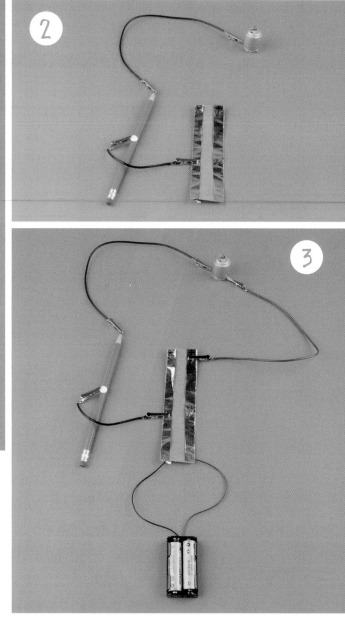

1. Ask an adult to push a thumbtack into the center of a wooden pencil. Attach a clip lead to the thumbtack. Connect this clip lead to one side of your circuit board.

2. Connect a second clip lead to the graphite at the tip of the pencil. Clip the other end of this to one terminal on the motor. Connect the other motor terminal to the other side of the circuit board with another clip lead.

3. Now connect your battery pack to the circuit board as you've done in the previous projects. Does the motor spin? How fast does it spin?

4. If the motor doesn't spin, check the circuit without the pencil resistor. With the resistor out of the circuit, the motor should spin fast. Make sure the clip leads are touching the pencil lead and try again. If it still doesn't work, move the thumbtack or nail closer to the tip of the pencil. Doing this will reduce the resistance, increase the current, and increase the motor speed.

WHAT HAPPENED?

The electric current had to pass, not only along the aluminum strips and clip leads, but also through the graphite in the pencil. The motor should spin slower than it did before because the circuit has higher resistance.

AC VS. DC

Batteries supply the electric energy we use in all these projects. The current flows from one battery terminal and through the circuit. Then it returns to the other terminal of the battery. This one-way current is called direct current or DC. The electricity you use from a wall outlet at home is not direct current. This current moves forward and backward very quickly. It is called alternating current or AC. AC is easier to transport at high voltages for long distances. So it makes sense to power buildings that way. DC is easier to create in small amounts, so it makes sense for batteries to be powered by DC.

Power lines carry
AC current long distances.

Challenge

You made a resistor out of a pencil. Can you guess which other
materials around you conduct electricity and which are insulators?
Does a colored pencil conduct electricity? What about a strip of
paper? Scissor blades? See what other materials you can put into
your circuit in place of the pencil. Does the motor spin? What else
can you try to use as a resistor?

CHAPTER 5

SWITCH IT ON AND OFF

When the room is dark, you flip a switch to turn on lights. But do you know how the switch works?

A switch is simply a device that can interrupt the flow of electrons. When a switch is turned on, the circuit is closed, and electrons flow. Engineers say the circuit is complete. When the switch off, the circuit is open, and electrons don't flow. You stay in the dark.

There are many different kinds of switches. When you flip the switch on the wall to light the lights, the lights stay on. Some wall switches not only turn lights on, but they also let you adjust how bright they are. Other switches keep the light on only as long as you push the switch. Some switches have a built-in timer that will turn off the circuit after a few minutes. Toasters have timed switches. Burglar alarms are switches that turn on lights or sound makers when a window or door opens. Heaters and refrigerators use switches that turn on and off depending on the temperature. Refrigerators also have switches that turn on the light inside.

Take a look around your home.
How many switches can you spot?

MAKE A SWITCH

What kind of switch do you think will work with the circuit you've made? Try making one that will start the motor running when you close the circuit. All you need are a few common items.

MATERIALS

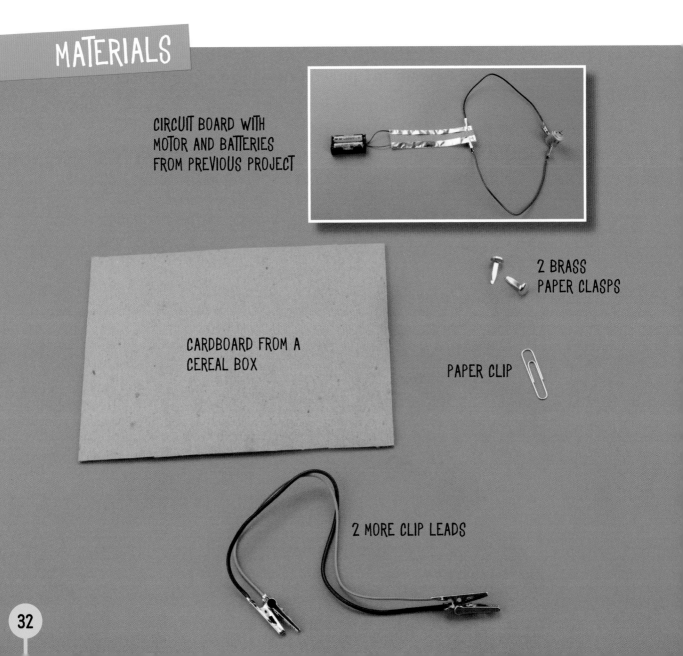

CIRCUIT BOARD WITH
MOTOR AND BATTERIES
FROM PREVIOUS PROJECT

2 BRASS
PAPER CLASPS

CARDBOARD FROM A
CEREAL BOX

PAPER CLIP

2 MORE CLIP LEADS

1 Cut a square of cardboard about 5 by 5 inches (13 by 13 cm).

2 Poke a hole in the cardboard, and push the first brass paper clasp through the hole. Spread the legs underneath to hold it in place.

3 Use the paper clip to estimate how far away the second brass clasp should be. You want the paper clip to be able to reach from one brass clasp to the other.

4 Poke the second hole. Hold the paper clip over the hole. Push the brass clasp through the end of the paper clip. Then push it into the hole in the cardboard and spread the legs of the brass clasp on the other side of the cardboard.

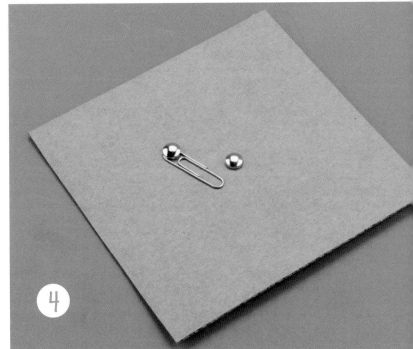

5 Now connect one end of a clip lead to one of the brass clasps. Connect the other end to the circuit. Connect your battery pack to the other brass clasp and to the circuit. You've made a switch!

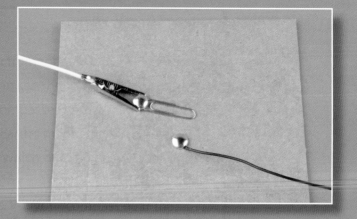

6 Insert the toy motor into the circuit. Slide the paper clip so it touches both brass clasps to make the motor spin. Slide it away to stop the motor.

When the paper clip touches both of the brass clasps electricity can flow through the circuit. The motor spins. When the clip is slid so it doesn't touch the second clasp, electricity cannot pass through the circuit so the motor stops. What if you wanted the motor to spin only when you were holding the switch closed? That requires a different kind of switch.

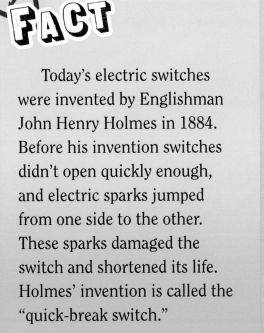

FACT

Today's electric switches were invented by Englishman John Henry Holmes in 1884. Before his invention switches didn't open quickly enough, and electric sparks jumped from one side to the other. These sparks damaged the switch and shortened its life. Holmes' invention is called the "quick-break switch."

MAKE A MOMENTARY CONTACT SWITCH

To make a switch that turns off when you release it you need a material that springs back. This type of switch is called a momentary contact switch. You might call it a push-button switch or a spring switch. A strip of metal from a disposable pie pan works great. Make sure to wash it first.

MATERIALS

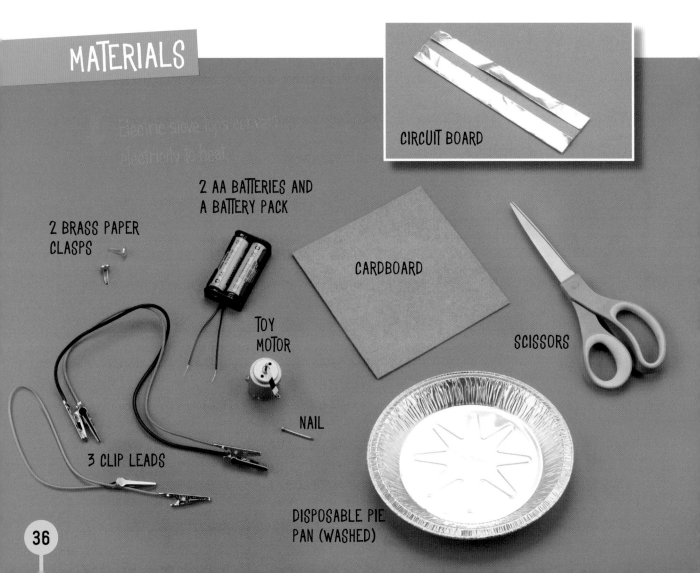

CIRCUIT BOARD

2 BRASS PAPER CLASPS

2 AA BATTERIES AND A BATTERY PACK

CARDBOARD

SCISSORS

TOY MOTOR

NAIL

3 CLIP LEADS

DISPOSABLE PIE PAN (WASHED)

1   Cut a strip of aluminum from the pie pan about 2 inches (5 cm) long and 0.5 inch (1.3 cm) thick.

2   Bend the aluminum into the shape of a "U" with flattened edges at the top.

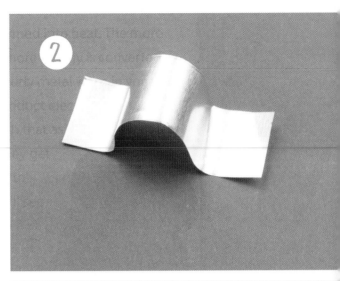

3   Ask an adult to poke a hole into one end of the metal strip using the nail.

4   Slide a brass clasp through the hole in the aluminum strip and into a piece of cardboard that is 5 inches (13 cm) on all sides.

5   Bend the aluminum strip so the other end stays above the cardboard.

6   Make a hole in the cardboard for a brass clasp directly beneath this end of the aluminum strip.

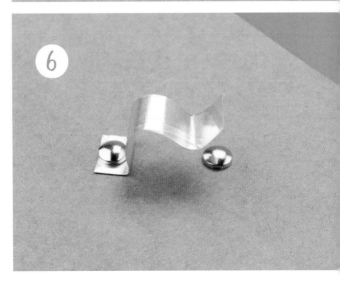

7 Connect clip leads to the two brass clasps and insert this switch into your circuit with the motor.

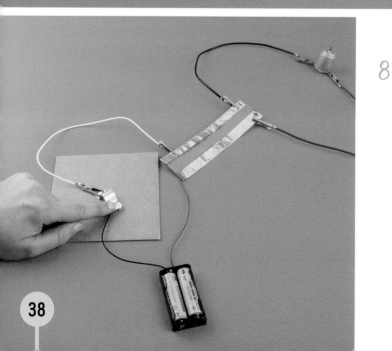

8 Push down on the aluminum strip so it touches the second brass clasp. The motor should spin. When you lift your finger, the circuit opens and the motor stops spinning.

Challenge

Make a Burglar Alarm Switch

You just made two switches that turned on a motor when you closed the switches. If you had an electric buzzer, those switches could have made a sound when you closed the circuit.

How would you design a circuit to make a sound if someone opened a door? The switch would have to close when the door opens. There are several ways to do this. One is to make a switch that will close when an insulator is pulled out. The insulator could be a piece of cereal box cardboard. It separates two brass clasps. When the insulator is pulled out by the door opening, the brass clasps touch. The buzzer sounds. Can you make a switch like this?

How else could you build a circuit so it would let you know when someone comes into a room?

HINT

To build a different type of alarm switch, look for a reed switch. Reed switches use magnets to turn circuits on and off.

CHAPTER 6

POWERING THE WORLD WITH ELECTRICITY

The AC electricity you get from wall outlets is made by giant motors called generators. To spin the generator motor shafts, power companies burn coal, oil, or gas. They may also use wind **turbines** or water turbines. Some use **nuclear** reactions to boil water. The water turns to steam and drives the blades of turbines. All these methods use different forces to spin a generator. The generator then creates electricity. You can create your own mini generator with toy motors.

turbine—a machine with blades that can be turned by a moving fluid such as steam or water

nuclear—having to do with the energy created by splitting atoms

MAKE ELECTRICITY

MATERIALS

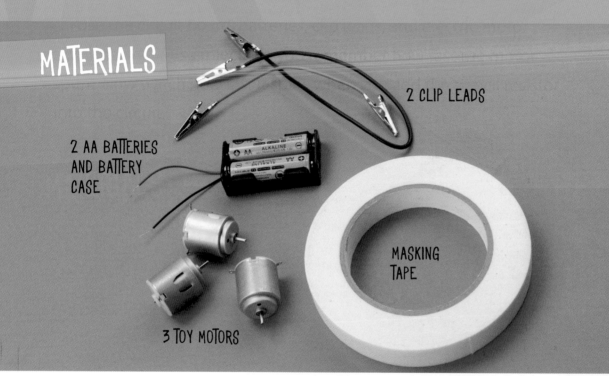

2 CLIP LEADS

2 AA BATTERIES
AND BATTERY
CASE

MASKING
TAPE

3 TOY MOTORS

STEPS

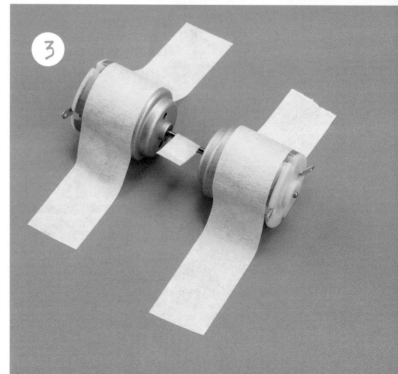

3

1 Set the two motors on a flat
   surface facing each other.
   The motor shafts should
   almost touch.

2 Tape each motor to the table.

3 Use a short piece of tape to hold
   the two motor shafts together.

4 Connect the terminal of one motor to a battery or battery pack. It should spin.

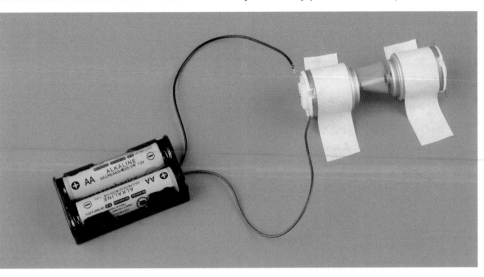

5 If you connect the terminals of the second motor to the terminals of the third motor, that motor will spin. The electricity you create in the second motor will power the third motor. In other words, the third motor is connected to a source of electricity just like the first motor is. The second motor is generating electricity when its shaft is turned by the shaft of the first motor.

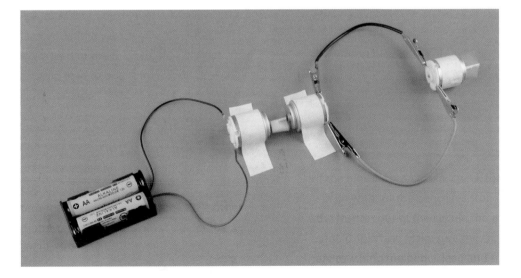

Do you remember how fast the first motor sounded? Did it slow down when you connected the third motor? How fast is the third motor spinning?

CHAPTER 7

STAY CHARGED UP!

If you enjoyed experimenting with electricity, then electrical engineering may be the career for you. To continue learning along this path, you need to take all the math and physics classes you can. And you need to build things. Hands-on work is a huge part of electrical engineering. See if your school has a robotics team or any other hands-on after-school programs you could join. If it has to do with math or science, it's a great opportunity to get involved.

Once you've completed high school, look for a college that offers a degree in electronics engineering. Many electronics engineers go beyond a four-year college degree and pursue masters' degrees. Electrical engineers are also required to take exams to stay up-to-date in their field. If you become an electrical engineer, the learning never stops. Advancements in technology happen all the time. Perhaps one of them will happen because of you.

GLOSSARY

atom (AT-uhm)—an element in its smallest form

circuit (SUHR-kuht)—a path for electricity to flow through

conductor (kuhn-DUHK-tuhr)—a material that lets heat, electricity, or sound travel easily through it

electron (i-LEK-tron)—a tiny particle in an atom that travels around the nucleus

insulator (IN-suh-late-ur)—a substance that prevents or reduces the passage of electricity

nuclear (NOO-klee-ur)—having to do with the energy created by splitting atoms

pole (POHL)—one of the two ends of a magnet

resist (ri-ZIST)—to oppose or slow the motion of an object

resistor (ri-ZISS-tuhr)—a tool or device that slows down the flow of electrons in a circuit with a resistant material

shaft (SHAFT)—a rotating rod that transmits power

solenoid (SOE-luh-noyd)—a coil of wire that acts as a magnet when carrying an electrical current

turbine (TUR-bine)—a machine with blades that can be turned by a moving fluid such as steam or water

volt (VOLT)—a unit for measuring the force of an electrical current or the stored power of a battery

READ MORE

Hayes, Amy. Freaky *Stories about Electricity*. Freaky True Science. New York: Gareth-Stevens Publishing, 2017.

Rohan, Rebecca Carey. *Working with Electricity: Electrical Engineers*. Engineers Rule! New York: PowerKids Press, 2016.

Sobey, Edwin J.C. *The Motorboat Book: Build & Launch 20 Jet Boats, Paddle-Wheelers, Electric Submarines & More*. Science in Motion. Chicago: Chicago Review Press, 2013.

MAKER SPACE TIPS

Download tips and tricks for using this book and others in a library maker space.

Visit *www.capstonepub.com/dabblelabresources*

INTERNET SITES

Use Facthound to find Internet sites related to this book.

Visit *www.facthound.com*

Just type in 9781515764267 and go.

Check out projects, games and lots more at
www.capstonekids.com

INDEX

AUTHOR BIO

Ed Sobey, PhD, is a world explorer with many scientific expeditions and a PhD in oceanography. He teaches oceanography and weather and climate for Semester at Sea.

Ed is a global evangelist for creative learning. He encourages creativity, inventing, and innovation through his books, workshops, and traveling museum exhibits. The Institute for International Education has awarded Ed two Fulbright grants for science teaching. Teachers in more than 30 countries have participated in his workshops.

He was the founding director of the National Inventors Hall of Fame, founder of the National Toy Hall of Fame, and co-founder of Kids Invent! He has directed five museums in the United States and has served as President of the Ohio Museums Association. He has also hosted two television shows on science for kids.